SAFE
PLACE
TO
GROW

SAFE PLACE TO GROW

Memories of a Childhood in Dublin, Ireland

OLIVE SPEIDEL HALL

TATE PUBLISHING & Enterprises

Published by Tate Publishing & Enterprises, LLC
127 E. Trade Center Terrace | Mustang, Oklahoma 73064 USA
1.888.361.9473 | www.tatepublishing.com

Tate Publishing is committed to excellence in the publishing industry. The company reflects the philosophy established by the founders, based on Psalm 68:11,
"The Lord gave the word and great was the company of those who published it."

Published in the United States of America

ISBN: 978-1-61777-317-4
1. Biography & Autobiography / General
2. Biography & Autobiography / Religious
11.04.21

DEDICATION

Dedicated to all the parents who take up the challenge of rearing their children in the nurture and admonition of the Lord. And to all the boys and girls who have the inestimable blessing of growing up in these homes.

Acknowledgments

I will always appreciate the devoted care my husband has given me since our marriage over forty-eight years ago. I am thankful for his patience through all the days of writing this book.

Our younger daughter, Barbara, and her husband and two children moved near us in 2005. I asked her if she could help me find a publisher for Safe Place to Grow. I do not know what I would have done without Barbara's help and the patience she has had with me as we completed this book. I have appreciated her keen interest in writing, in publishing, and in the sharing of her computer skills.

I would like especially to thank Ashley Luckett at Tate for her professional, kind attention to the editing of my manuscript. Also, I appreciate Kristen Verser's attention to detail in the cover design. Christina Hicks has been so gracious in laying out my book so nicely. My thanks to my dear friend Jeanie Hartman for her original art on the cover. My thanks to my lifelong friend Paula Crawford for taking the time to write the foreword. My thanks to my friend Willette Ericson for reading through my manuscript and seeing corrections that had passed me by.

TABLE OF CONTENTS

FOREWORD

My first introduction to the Speidel family was in a church service in Colorado Springs. We had heard that a new family was coming from Ireland, and there they were—all ten of them—sitting in the very front pew! That wasn't the usual location for a family with eight young children, especially considering the youngest was an infant. So I observed them with interest. Throughout the entire service, which must have continued for an hour and a half, there they sat, perfectly quiet and well behaved. Now I understood why the parents had the courage to sit in the front pew.

In later years, Olive came into my life. She was an attractive, vivacious girl with a ready smile. This was the beginning of a lifelong friendship that I cherish deeply. With character that reflects her upbringing, she has been a precious influence in my life and, for over fifty years, has been an honest, loving, dependable, and faithful friend. Over the years, we have shared our joys and sorrows, even when separated by many miles.

One summer, the Speidel family invited me to spend a few days at a rustic cabin with them. They were such a happy family bound together by loving parents. Each child had his or her appointed tasks that were carried out with goodwill. One made a large batch of yeast bread, and others washed dishes, carried in wood for the fire, or swept the floor. Then came family prayers, led by Mr. Speidel. This wasn't a dull, tedious exercise, but one filled with the sense of the love of God. Mr. Speidel not only prayed for his sons and daughters but with them. Then there was time for fun, hiking, and exploring in the beautiful Colorado mountains.

Mr. and Mrs. Speidel were obviously not only loved but also respected by this family of bright, gifted children. Music had a large place in their lives, and while it was a means of great enjoyment, disciplined practice enabled them to perform with skill. Whatever they undertook to do, they were expected to do it well.

In this collection of memories, entitled Safe Place to Grow, I believe Olive has sought to reveal glimpses of her family's life that can be useful to other families. How foreign such a childhood is to most children today. Much of the Old World way of life is now long gone, but still there are parents who reject potentially damaging modern-day influences as they strive to bring up their children in a more wholesome environment. Olive's life as a child may be considered quaint by many, but her experience could be a model for Christian parents who want their children to have a better life. To these children, I commend these vignettes of a lively little Irish girl.

—Paula Crawford

PREFACE

I have read and heard of so many children who had been abused behind closed doors as they were growing up. I have had the deepest compassion for these precious little people. However, I realized that there were countless parents all over the world who were trying to raise their children lovingly and wisely and that I felt I must write about my own memories so that these families would know they are not alone. There have always been parents like them, and there always will be. This book is a collection of memories from my childhood, sharing the love that I experienced with the hope today's parents will be encouraged to nurture the innocence of children.

PROLOGUE

Daddy was Eric Gottlieb Speidel. His grandfather was John Speidel. Great-granddad's brother had been killed in the Franco-Prussian War. Great-granddad's mother didn't want to lose another son, so she sent Great-granddad to England with a Bible and a silver coin. He settled in Lancaster where he married Polly Douthwaite. Granddad Speidel was their first child. Great-granddad Speidel went into the pork business. When Granddad grew up, he married beautiful Jennie Townley, and they moved to Dublin, Ireland, to start up the pork business there. Great-grandad moved with them. When he passed away, he owned the entire block of homes where he lived. All this was profit from a Bible, one silver piece, and a Christian life.

Granddad Speidel raised his children at Belleview on Merrion Road. Daddy was the oldest of six children, all of whom were christened at Abbey Street Methodist Church.

INTRODUCTION

Ireland is divided into two parts. The six counties of Ulster, the province in the North, are predominantly Protestant and are governed by England. Belfast is the capital of the North of Ireland. The rest of the counties in the south compose the Republic of Ireland and are predominantly Catholic; Dublin, the capital city, is a metropolitan city situated on the east coast; the River Liffey opens into the Irish Sea making Dublin a busy seaport. Trinity College is its main college, and nearby is the University of Dublin. Interestingly, each Protestant denomination has its own high school.

First Awareness of Life

Someone was trying to put my Wellington boots on my fast-growing feet. I was crying because my beloved little red boots simply would not push on. After I was helped down from the white enamel back porch table, Audrey and I walked down the wide driveway, hand in hand. We sisters were always together; Audrey is twenty-one months older than me.

Our family had been evacuated from Marino Mart on the north side of Dublin to a farmhouse in Kilmurry, south of Dublin. Daddy had gone to work in the North Strand on his motorbike one morning only to find rubble remaining where the family meat business had stood the day before. A German bomb had found its target on the night of May 30-31, 1941.[1] Granddad Speidel had been sending barrels of meat to England. The Nazis put an end to that. There were always three shops, until the war. After the bombing, the meat-processing space was moved to the back of the Marino Mart shop; a third shop was opened again in the Strand across from the original main store.

Our spirits were happy; our white pinafores were freshly starched; the sun was shining as we strolled along the path. A deep well caught my attention. How clear and cold the still water was, and looking through a break in the hedge behind it, one of the fat cows from Joseph's dream gently mooed as her eyes met mine. At teatime that evening, we girls were amazed to hear how the fresh eggs were being stolen from the henhouse. Daddy explained that a rat lay on his back, held the egg in his four paws, and the other rats pulled him and the egg to their nest for a feast.

Daddy and Mother decided it was safe to return home to Marino Mart, where our two-story flat was situated above the new meat shop there. Audrey and I stood on the seat, gazing out the back window of the Hilman Minx. Daddy drove carefully as Mother cared for Jean and baby David in the front seat. How exciting to see the staff standing in their white aprons outside the front display window, smiling and waving, welcoming their beloved Eric and his family home.

I was in the crib in Daddy and Mother's room the day before I was nine months old. Mother wasn't quite sure what was happening when Jean was born in the afternoon. Mother sent Audrey downstairs to the shop to have Daddy come upstairs. He immediately took Jean to the Rotunda Hospital, where she was placed in an incubator—she was a preemie weighing three pounds. Aunt Emily was furious with Mother for allowing Audrey to come down to the shop to ask Daddy to come upstairs. Audrey had to walk out the front door of the flat on to the sidewalk in front of the display window to get into the shop. Aunt Emily was afraid Audrey would not know where to go or that someone might have bothered her.

Giggles and squeals were coming from the green room when Audrey and I were supposed to be sleeping. But no, we were taking turns jumping from the recessed windowsill on to the soft silk bedspread. Daddy walked in, gently took me in his arms and carried me across the hall to the blue room. He laid me down between the cool, clean sheets, and I was asleep before he had quietly closed the door.

Another day, Daddy's aunt, Emily Townley, was visiting for lunch. Aunt Emily worked for Daddy in the meat shop downstairs. Daddy was the apple of her eye. I was too keyed up to nap in Daddy and Mother's rose room. Instead, I was jumping up and down on the silky-soft eiderdown. I suddenly catapulted off the bed and cut the bridge of my nose as I crashed into the brass knob on the dresser drawer. The scar stayed for years as a reminder.

Mealtime in our family took different forms. In the earliest years, I enjoyed watching Mother clear the ashes from the grate in the kitchen fireplace each morning; peace filled the house while Mother cooked porridge for breakfast on the gas stove. At times Mother spent cherished time with us as we learned by watching her work, but at other times we adjusted to various staff in our home, whom Daddy and Mother employed to help with the cooking or housekeeping as the family grew.

One Easter Sunday afternoon, Audrey and I stood at a dining room chair, tasting the delicious Cadbury Easter eggs we were given. How pretty they were, decorated with pink flowers and green leaves. Our heads and shoulders came just above the seat of the dining room chair.

We were still quite small when our family was staying in a rented house in Howth for a summer holiday. Mother wasn't feeling well one morning; so Daddy said he would brush my long brown curls. I climbed under the white enamel breakfast table and would not come out to have those tangles brushed out, so my hair did not get brushed that day.

About this time, the Sunday school had a social in the fellowship hall. The parents were sitting lovingly on the front rows of chairs near the stage. I got up to say my Sunday school piece.

"Mother, Mother, I am sick. Send for the doctor, quick, quick, quick!"

Everybody dissolved in laughter. I am sure this was not my assigned piece; I probably just got up and said it, possibly making it up on the spot. Audrey stood up to say her piece but melted immediately into tears and found refuge in Mother's lap.

A wicker Moses basket appeared in the living room. We had a beautiful ginger-haired baby sister named Grace Freda. She was so quiet and sweet.

First Days of School

Audrey was five. It was time for her to start school. Mother did not think Audrey was brave enough to start by herself, so she enrolled me as well. Since Mother was not well the first day we attended, her twin sister, Auntie Gladys, took us to the Presbyterian elementary school about a block north of our home. As soon as Auntie Gladys left, Audrey went to the door, jumping up as she tried to reach the doorknob, crying to go home. I was placed in a different classroom after that to help Audrey adjust.

We heard that when our daddy was born, his grandfather promised Daddy a house if he were named for him. My grandparents gave Daddy his grandfather's name, Gottlieb, for a middle name, and Great-granddad did finance our first home. In the autumn of 1942, we moved to 32 Kincora Road, Clontarf.

Paddy was a crippled man who came to visit regularly. Mother always had him come in to the kitchen for a cup of tea. He was a gentleman, and we children enjoyed gathering around to talk to him for the few minutes he stayed. One day, he told us he was getting married, and as young as I was, I could understand someone wanting to marry this gracious, soft-spoken gentleman with the clear skin and kind brown eyes. Paddy didn't need to visit after he was married.

About this time, one morning, I was all bent out of shape about something and decided I would run away from home. I walked past the four houses to our right and went down Oulton Road. I was about halfway down Oulton Road when I saw Daddy's red business van driving on Clontarf Road, delivering the daily order of fresh sausages, hams, and bacon from Marino Mart to the shop on Clontarf Road near Vernon Avenue. The clear sign, J. Speidel and Sons Ltd., painted in black on the side brought me back to my senses, and I soberly turned around and walked home again.

Mrs. McAllister very ably played the organ for church, but I was sure she was getting too old because the leaders' board hired a fine young divinity student from Trinity College. Noel was shy, refined, and had wavy golden hair. I looked up to him with total respect.

Each St. Patrick's Day, Mother wrapped an ivory bone bachelor's button and a bone ring in tissue paper and hid them in the mashed potatoes for dinner. Whoever got the ring would surely marry; whoever got the bachelor's button would not. Some of Mother's friends sent tiny damp shamrocks in a small white gift box through the mail. Ireland is the only place in the world where the tiny shamrocks grow.

Abbey Street Methodist Church found the Speidels sitting in their own pew every Sunday morning. One Sunday, a homeless man came in and sat in the back pew. When Holy Communion was served, he went to the front and knelt with the church members to be served. The rank and file were disgraced that he was there with them. Daddy and Mother commented later that they thought he had a right to be there if he chose.

Greenlanes School

Greenlanes School was situated on Seafield Avenue down the road from St. John's Episcopal Church. Greenlanes was a national school. Dublin had Protestant schools and Catholic schools. Across the road from Greenlanes, a Catholic school was completely enclosed behind high, stucco walls. Greenlanes was a Protestant school; the teachers in Greenlanes attended St. John's Episcopal Church. We could see the steeple on St. John's from the front of our home. One year, we were giving a school concert in Greenlanes. I must have been in one of the infant classes because I was waiting in the wings on a stick horse, ready to ride in, as the class sang, "Ride a Cockhorse to Banbury Cross." Because of dreaminess, I missed my cue, and Mrs. Freyer swatted me on the backside to remind me to get going.

Audrey and I were enrolled in Greenlanes National School. Even though I was still too young to be put on the roll, we were in a real class setting, learning to read, write, and recognize our numbers. A few grades later, a large entrance room to the school was a great place for the class to sit on the steps and recite our tables: "Four ones are four; four twos are ei-eight..." in a singsong manner.

In Greenlanes School, each one of us had six-inch knitting needles and learned to knit. At home, Audrey and I would cuddle into Mother while she helped us make some progress on our project. Later we advanced to using four needles and learned to knit socks. What an accomplishment it was to turn a heel. When I was twelve, I enjoyed knitting a light-blue sweater. I had a slip stitch in the pattern after each set of six purl stitches. I made a mistake and put the slip stitch either before or after the proper place. I didn't correct the mistake and wore the sweater with that fault in it.

Mrs. Spearman taught third and fourth class. She was motherly, very beautiful, slightly plump, and seemed always to wear a lovely copen-blue striped wool suit. She kept perfect order in her classroom without even trying. Her teaching was of the highest quality, and she was never tired. I well remember parsing sentences: common and proper nouns, definite and indefinite articles, adjectives and adverbs.

In school, we were studying the history of Ireland. We heard that Brian Boru[2], who had become the High King of Ireland, had held off Norsemen by the Irish Sea,[2] which we could see from our back bedroom windows. Brian Boru's sword, we read, was hanging in Clontarf Castle. The sword was displayed in the hall of the great estate that was situated at the end of our road. We learned that the castle was the only Tudor castle in the country of Ireland and that the tower was built in AD 900. After school, without thinking to ask if I could go over there, I walked up to the great oak front door of the Tudor Castle and knocked. A maid in a black dress, frilly white apron, and cap opened the front door.

"May I see Brian Boru's sword?" I asked politely.

"No," she answered and firmly closed the huge door.

In Greenlanes School, whenever the headmaster walked into our classroom, all of us children stood briefly and said, in singsong manner, "Good morning, sir!" On Wednesdays, the rector from St. John's Episcopal Church came to give a short devotional in our classroom. We respected him highly. In fifth class, he came once each week on Wednesday mornings and taught us the Apostle Paul's missionary journeys from the Book of Acts, using a fine map as he taught.

Mr. Spearman was the headmaster of Greenlanes. He taught fifth and sixth classes. Our classroom was on the platform of the large assembly hall. A horizontally slatted wall folded down from the ceiling to make a nice classroom up there. Before I moved into his class, he came to see his wife for some brief business reason in the classroom in the assembly hall. Fifth and sixth class started a low mumble of chatter while he was gone. He strode over to the platform and rattled the stacked chairs against the slatted wall. "Seniors! Seniors!" he yelled. And quietness was restored.

While we were attending school at Greenlanes, several of us children had the measles. Mother put up the blackout curtains at the windows to protect our eyes. She said they had used them during the war. I awakened in the middle of the night, and my eyes would not open; they were glued shut. "I'm blind! I'm blind!" I shouted with visions of the blind people Jesus had healed vividly portrayed in my mind. Daddy came in to see what was wrong. He dampened a facecloth and gently daubed my eyes until I could open them again. "I can see! I can see!" I cried with relief.

I liked to quietly watch Mother come home from a social engagement. I sat on her bed and watched her take off her engagement ring; she put it in a large walnut jewelry box that sat on top of Daddy's short wardrobe. I could tell she treasured her ring and also her marriage to Daddy. Then she would take off her fox fur and place it carefully on the shelf in her wardrobe. Next, she would take off her lovely brown suit and hang it on a hanger and place that in the wardrobe. I knew that a salesman had come into the shop and sold Daddy the brown-striped wool for Mother and grey-striped wool for him, and they had their suits custom tailored.

Daddy came home for dinner each workday. It was served at one o'clock by the dining room fire for Daddy and Mother. We children ate in the kitchen, accompanied by the housekeeper. Many, many times I have seen Mother and Daddy wrapped in a long embrace in the dining room doorway before Daddy would return to work. If I ran down the stairs when Daddy was coming out of the dining room, he would hold out his arms and I would run into his warm embrace while he said, "Daddy loves his girlies." The button on his suit jacket pressed into my cheek, but I didn't mind because I knew I was being loved.

Olive Speidel Hall

During the war, Daddy dug up the lawns in the front and back gardens and planted potatoes. This was our victory garden. When the potatoes were ready to harvest, Daddy dug a deep hole, in which he placed a shallow layer of straw. Next, he placed a layer of potatoes. He repeated this process until all the potatoes were safely protected for the winter.

Daddy had bought Mother three boxes of Cadbury's Milk Tray chocolates: a three-pound, a two-pound, and a one-pound. She had them stacked on her wardrobe shelf. When nobody noticed, I would slip up to their room and reach up to those boxes and help myself to those chocolates. Relishing one led to taking a second, then a third. I had done this more than once when Mother asked, "Olive, have you been stealing my chocolates?"

"I just took one," I lied. Mother reported this wickedness to Daddy. When he came home for his dinner break, he called me to the dining room and told me how bad this was and that he would have to punish me. He placed me facedown over his knee and spanked me gently on my behind. I could see David peering worriedly in the French door window while he cupped his hands around his eyes to block out the sunshine's glare. I was so ashamed that I could not go back out to play; I went upstairs to David's bedroom. It was small, and I thought nobody would bother me there. I lay down on the bed with my face to the wall. I heard

Daddy come in and heard him call my name. I was so hurt that I wouldn't turn around to look at him. He put his hand on my left shoulder and gently turned me around to look at him. "You know Daddy loves you, don't you?" How could I doubt it?

I went through a phase where I liked playing tricks on Mother. One afternoon I tied the end of a black spool of thread to the fastener on the window in Daddy and Mother's bedroom; I let the spool fall to the grass below. I went downstairs and took the spool to the front door knocker. I tied the thread to the knocker and went upstairs again. I pulled gently on the black thread to make the door knocker work. Mother went to the door and, of course, couldn't see anybody. After a little while, I tried again. Mother went to the door again and thought she was hearing things. I was very amused upstairs.

Another day, I wrote her a letter and mailed it. I pretended to be a friend and wrote that I was coming to visit on a certain day. She believed the letter and talked about it. Of course, I didn't follow through but was delighted that I had fooled Mother.

My sister Enid was ready for bed. As we were gathered around the fireplace in the dining room, Enid was standing too close to the fire, and her long flannel gown caught fire. Mother pushed her own chair back and pulled Enid to the rug in front of the fireplace.

She quickly wrapped Enid in the rug and the fire was put out. However, Enid had bad burns on her legs.

I can still in my mind's eye see the long blisters on her leg when Dr. May came to check on her at home. Good care eventually healed her burns. They say "a burned child dreads the fire." Well, this wasn't true for Enid, because another time her dress caught fire at the dining room fireplace and she went running for the front door, with flames burning up her back. Susan, our housekeeper, stopped her and got the fire patted out. I believe her beautiful ash brown curls were singed.

During the war, an air-raid siren would go off loudly at the end of Kincora Road. Freda was under three years old, and she would understandably always start crying as she ran for the back door. Simultaneously, the back porch door would open and Mother would gather her in her arms to comfort her. When we looked up at any airplane going over during those days, we were sure we saw the black swastika emblazoned on the belly of the plane.

I recall I was late to school only one time. I was not aware that I was returning late after lunch until I saw the schoolyard empty, the cloakroom full of coats, and noticed the total absence of student chatter. When I opened the classroom door, the afternoon session had already started. Mrs. Spearman was tossing the penmanship books on the desk space in front of each student. She commented that my penmanship was below par that day. I knew I was deeply embarrassed to be late.

Our places in the classroom were assigned in accordance with how our grades averaged out at the end of the term. Except for one time, Barbara Fox always averaged the highest, so she sat on the back seat in the first place. Barbara was a sweet, slightly plump, and quiet girl with long, soft brown ringlets. When Ronnie Tucker took first place, Barbara cried quietly. I usually placed third in the class of twenty-six, but I was delighted when I edged Ronnie Tucker into third place and I took second place.

Mrs. Spearman was out of the room momentarily when one of the girls went up and sat at the teacher's desk, picking up Mrs. Spearman's ruler and pretending to play teacher. She said some unforgettably vulgar words, and just then, Mrs. Spearman pulled open the sliding door to return. This student scooted back to her desk, and Mrs. Spearman wisely ignored the situation. She was a very pretty girl with soft, short brown curls. Her father's job was to deliver coal in the area; her mother lacked refinement, and I felt sorry that day for the daughter because she had tried to gain attention in school in that fashion.

A lane went from Greenlanes School to Kincora Road, which followed beside the Catholic school. We always went to and from school on the lane that went up between St. John's Episcopal Church and the rectory. I do not know what possessed Audrey, Jean, and me to walk down the lane by the Catholic school. As we were walking toward our home, a group of Catholic boys held hands and strung across the street and side-walks and intimidated us about passing. We were very frightened. They seemed so much bigger than we were. Audrey took my hand and Jean's hand and rushed the boys in a wonderfully stubborn way. Fortunately, we broke through.

Another time, we Speidel girls and the Stein girls were waiting outside the side door at Clontarf Methodist Church; Mr. Brien had not come yet to open the door. A group of boys came and chased us back behind the church into the bushes. One of them scared Joan very badly. She was very shaken, under-standably, as we walked home after Christian Endeavor. We didn't recognize these boys from church or school and concluded they were Catholic boys. There were no street gangs in Dublin that I can remember.

By this time, Audrey had transferred to Wesley College. Her uniform was a red, long-sleeved rayon shirt; navy, white, and red-striped tie; navy gymslip; and long, red, woven girdle tied around the waist. She wore a navy cardigan, long, black, cotton stockings, and black Oxford shoes. She wore a navy tam with the Wesley crest on the front and a navy gabardine coat. It was our first separation. That night, I awakened with Daddy's hand gently on my shoulder. I was walking in my sleep through the kitchen with her long, black stockings wrapped around my neck. Daddy gently led me back to bed and tucked me in safely.

One year, we had a beautiful girl from Tipperary for our maid. She worked hard, and I thought she had lovely manners. Mother encouraged her to join the Salvation Army, and she looked very attractive in her army uniform. Mother let her take us to visit her beautiful baby, John, at the Bethany Home, where she had lived for a short time before she came to work for us. One day, I was so shocked to hear this beautiful girl crying. I peeked into the drawing room, and Mother was sitting by our beloved maid, comforting her. Two cups of tea were sitting on the Queen Anne tea table, which had been drawn up close to the sofa. Mother whispered to me later that our beloved maid had just given her baby up for adoption.

A lovely group portrait of Great-aunt Alice's wedding was framed and hung over the fireplace in our bedroom on Kincora Road. The ladies wore large straw hats swathed in matching tulle. I wakened, screaming that these hats had changed into motorcars and were coming straight for me to run over me. Daddy came in, wrapped me in a blanket, and carried me downstairs, where he and Mother were sitting cozily by the fire. He held me on his lap for a while until the fright was gone, and then he carried me back to bed and tucked me in.

One of the other Salvation Army lassies was planning a wedding. We children really liked her and her fiancé. Audrey and I were delighted when the couple asked us to sing at their wedding reception. They made their home in a delightful first-floor flat near Greenlanes School. Audrey and I enjoyed visiting them, especially when they had twins a year later.

The last house on the left side of Haddon Road was a Salvation Army guest house. Major Acton was the stout, cheerful matron. I liked to stop in to see her sometimes. One day when we were standing in her dining room, the telephone rang. When Major Acton reached to pick up the phone, the chair she intended to sit on scooted away from her and she slipped down on the floor. She laughed long and heartily before she was able to start her phone conversation.

About this time, the Salvation Army was having some special services. A visiting band from England was some of their guests. Our family kept one of the trombonists. We were fascinated as we watched him practice in our dining room. His wit intrigued us when he called his trombone his "come back and I'll fetch you."

On Sunday evenings, the YMCA conducted evangelical services, which followed the regular church evening services. After the war, we were attending a service there. Pastor Martin Nieomuller came through a door on the right-hand side gallery and walked toward the railing; he waved to us. He was gaunt from being imprisoned in a concentration camp for the last seven years of the Nazis' rule. We were so moved to see him.

Another Sunday evening, the founders of the Salvation Army, William and Catharine Booth's daughter gave a talk about her work in Paris. She was called "the Marechale" and was dressed in robes very much like Mother Teresa wore. The Stuart Watt ladies were sitting on the platform behind the Marechal. After about one and one-half hours of a spellbinding speech, one of them leaned forward and tugged on her robe to hint that it was time to close her talk. The Misses Clara and Eva Stuart Watt presided over a homeless shelter on Eden Quay. They lived about one mile northwest of our home. Their brother was a missionary in Africa, and the ladies had an African hut made out of concrete in their back yard. Once when their brother was visiting, Audrey and I were invited to have tea around a table in the African hut.

We were learning singular and plural tenses in school. Uncle Barton was putting some cash in the safe, which was well hidden from view under the coats in front of the door that led to our flat upstairs. I informed him that the plural of roof is roofs and the plural of calf is calves, but the plural of safe is not saves—saves is a verb. I wondered why he was smiling so honestly into my eyes. Later, Daddy told me that Uncle Barton was impressed with my knowledge of spelling and grammar.

Occasionally, I walked up Castle Avenue to Furry Park Road where Uncle Barton and Auntie Ann lived. Auntie Ann grew up in a Catholic family. She was a beautiful, gracious lady with raven, shoulder-length hair. She always welcomed me and served me lunch in her attractive kitchen. She invited me to browse through her women's magazines while her radio played music in the dining room. Uncle Barton and Auntie Ann attended Abbey Street Methodist Church every Sunday morning with their three attractive children: Adrienne, Trevor, and Leslie.

Uncle Barton bought a half-moon cherry wood console table for Auntie Ann, which she placed in the downstairs hall; she liked it very much. Uncle Barton painted all the inside passage doors white and then put a coat of pink on top, in which he made grain- like markings with a comb while the upper paint was still wet. Auntie Ann was very happy with this change of decor.

When Princess Elizabeth was married, the fifth and sixth classes joined us in the intermediate classes in the gymnasium, and we listened to her wedding, which was broadcast on the radio.

In another venue, the Catholic Church on Clontarf Road near Vernon Avenue was celebrating. The main priest was dressed in his vestments holding aloft "the Host," which was a sample of the bread and wine which was used during Holy Communion. The other priests were walking behind him, swinging incense burners. The nuns fell in step behind them, followed by many Catholic parishioners who proceeded to march around the block. Audrey, Jean, and I went down to see what was going on. All the Catholic people who gathered on the sidewalks kneeled down and genuflected as the

Host passed them by. Audrey, Jean, and I felt like the Three Hebrew Children.

When I was in fifth class, we had to study Gaelic definitions on the weekends. I had a special notebook in which I kept adding to them in my neatest handwriting. One of Mr. Spearman's rules was that we could not say "I forgot" if we came without our homework. One Monday morning, I didn't even notice I had forgotten to do my Irish meanings until Irish class began. "All those who do not have their Irish meanings copied, stand up."

I stood up, along with two or three others.

"Why do you not have your work done?" Mr. Spearman was standing near my desk.

"I didn't remember," I answered truthfully.

"Hold out your hand," Mr. Spearman ordered, and he caned my left hand angrily. The next day, my beloved Mrs. Spearman met me momentarily and sadly observed, "I heard you had to be caned yesterday." I have only recently realized that it was very soon after this episode that Daddy told me that he and Mother had enrolled me to start Wesley College after Christmas.

Whole Note, Half Note

Audrey and I started piano lessons when I was six years old. We were blessed to have Grandmother Price's old black upright piano in our dining room.

We walked half a mile to Miss Edith Daly's three-story house on Haddon Road. I thought Miss Daly was probably seventy years old; she was quaint, diminutive, the quintessential piano teacher. She taught piano during the school day at Wesley College, Dublin, and rode the bus home to teach private lessons in her old-world studio in the lovely English garden behind the house. A floral, chintz-covered bench sat against the entire south wall. Another matching bench sat against part of the west wall. The old upright piano sat somberly to the right against the west wall. A shelf up close to the ceiling on the south wall was stacked with music. The students sat on a walnut Queen Anne chair with a ruffle surrounding the floral-upholstered seat. While she taught, Miss Daly wore a dainty, black felt hat and generally drank a cup of hot tea from an English fine-bone china matched cup and saucer. She didn't know we could see her stockings rolled down onto inch-wide elastic garters just below her knees. She looked at us over the top of round, wire-rimmed glasses that perched on the end of her nose. A Queen Anne table sat in the right-hand corner. Miss Daly could control the rare Irish sunshine by drawing chintz curtains across the short, wide window behind her. Another chintz-curtained window gave ample light on the north wall.

Miss Daly was a member of the Royal Irish Academy of Music. Each spring, she arranged for her students to audition at the Shelbourne Hotel on St. Stephen's Green, with an academy judge visiting from England. Mother made it a gala day, and immediately following the auditions, she took us to Bewley's for coffee and a cream puff or artistically frosted miniature cake. The trip ended with a stop at the General Post Office[3] to visit Granddad Price in his international office.

Audrey and I highly regarded our fellow students at the studio: Ann and Joan Stein and Pamela and Maureen Wakely. We were amused when a short newspaper account told how well Derek Johnson had scored at his piano audition. "We did better," we whispered to each other, quite surprised. Miss Daly taught us time this way: a whole note was called a semibreve, a half-note was called a minim, a quarter note was a crotchet, an eighth note was a quaver, a sixteenth note was a semi-quaver, a thirty-second note was a semi-demi-quaver, and a sixty-fourth note was a semi-demi-semi-quaver.

Miss Daly taught us time very thoroughly. I can remember rippling those words off the end of our tongues without becoming tongue-tied.

We enjoyed arriving early at our lesson when we could hear the previous student playing his or her delightful pieces. I was very surprised when beautiful Maureen Wakely actually fastened the waistband of her pretty dirndl skirt with a safety pin. Miss Daly liked us. She smiled into our eyes sometimes when she taught us. One afternoon, she bustled in a little late. As she squeezed past the student chair, she told us she had forgotten her umbrella that rainy day. Well, she had handled that easily by dashing to the kitchen at Wesley College and grabbing a clean dish towel to tie over her hat to protect it from the rain.

Another lesson day, it was pouring rain outside when it was time for me to go home. "Stop and ask my sister for bus fare," advised Miss Daly. Obediently, I rapped at the backdoor. Miss Daly, the housekeeper, came back from somewhere with a sixpence.

"I'll bring you back the change," I acknowledged my thanks.

"Indeed! You'll bring me back the sixpence!" countered the other Miss Daly.

On Saturday afternoons, we gathered at the piano studio for theory class. If someone were not finished with his or her lesson, the rest of us would gather near the trellis among the roses and visit while we waited. An attractive stone wall around the property made the English garden quite secluded because of its height. Our headmaster at Greenlanes had just been coaching us to keep on our toes by correcting him if we caught him quoting some fact incorrectly. Sure enough, Miss

Daly said something incorrectly while she was standing teaching theory. Like lightning, up went my hand; I pointed out her error. Her eyes grew large, her hands gripped the edge of the Queen Anne chair, and I haven't corrected a teacher ever since!

Walking to piano lessons was ethereal. In the autumn, the leaves were crunchy on the sidewalk, I liked to slowly slide my right shoe along on the pavement until the leaves became a big pile and then start another in the same manner. Our journey took us past Clontarf Castle on the right and the residence of J. Bloodsmith, Solicitor, on the left. A high retaining wall and many stately trees hid the castle from immediate view. A high wall on the left protected the Bloodsmith Estate. The gold plaque on the left entrance pillar was impressive to a child. Often, one of the tall wrought-iron gates stood ajar.

About this time, Mrs. Rock was watching us children one day while Mother was gone. She was standing behind the closed kitchen door, wringing her hands, her face distorted with fear while she whispered a prayer. I was eager to see who this person could be that could cause such distress in Mrs. Rock's mind. I went upstairs and looked out the bay window in Daddy and Mother's room.

Just at that moment, a homeless man, still a few houses away, looked up at me and shook his fist threateningly as he caught my eye. No wonder Mrs. Rock was wringing her hands so despairingly downstairs.

Before Enid was born, we children took the kitchen chairs out on the back lawn and sat around in a circle, looking up at the sky, waiting for a baby to come down from heaven. Some days later, we were all five huddled together, sitting on the stairs under the landing window, softly crying. Mother was missing. We couldn't find her anywhere. We heard footsteps on the kitchen floor. Our crying crescendoed into loud wails as the door slowly opened. It was Daddy! Home in the middle of the afternoon. All of us ran down into his arms. "Why, children," he soothed, "your mother is in the hospital. I took her there myself."

A few days later, we came home from school for dinner. A surprise awaited. The pram was sitting in the dining room with a beautiful baby girl snuggled under a soft pink baby shawl. Mother was hiding behind the dining room door with a big smile on her face. She told us that this beautiful baby's name was Enid Patricia. We were so happy to have her in our family.

One Saturday evening, Daddy was sitting in his chair, choosing hymns for Sunday evening service. I was still quite small, and while leaning against his side, my head came under the arm of his chair. He was singing one of the hymns he was studying. I didn't realize I was singing with him. "Olive," he said, smiling, "I didn't know you could sing alto." I didn't know either. I just was.

Piano lessons were becoming very interesting. Mother didn't have to compel us to practice now. She had bought a brand new ebony piano from her cousin. What a beautiful tone it had, with shiny white ivories and solid black keys. Mother put this piano in the drawing room. Only Audrey and I were allowed to play it.

One day, I didn't notice I had lapsed into a dreamy mood. I was playing a piece I had never heard before. In etude style, I was playing broken chords coming up in the left hand meeting broken chords coming down in the right hand. It was a perfect piece with a nice ending. Mother was upstairs in the room above and called down, "Olive, that was lovely." Immediately, I came out of my reverie; I felt so guilty that I was not playing my assigned music. I knew Mother thought that solo was in one of my books.

I went right back to my studies. I was playing Chopin's "Minute Waltz" and a lovely solo Daddy had learned as a boy, "In a Monastery Garden." Audrey and I were playing a delightful French duet, "Chilperic." The music was old and brown, with some of the edges already splintering off.

Girls' Brigade

Abbey Street Methodist Church had a Girls' Brigade group that met each Saturday afternoon in the small church gymnasium. We practiced gym exercises set to music. The leader, Miss Williams, had been Mother's piano teacher when Mother was a girl. When I sat down and played a tune by ear, Miss Williams chided me. While I yearned to be in the Girl-Guides, Mother said we needed to be loyal to her piano teacher.

Mother's mother graduated from the Teachers' Training College, Dublin. This education department was a part of Trinity College, Dublin. It was under the auspices of the Church of Ireland. No Catholic schools would hire these graduates to teach in their schools.

One Saturday afternoon, all of the Girls' Brigade groups in the city gathered in the large gymnasium over Abbey Street Methodist Church. Each group had its own flag that was presented before they performed their routines. Besides aerobics, some of our routines were skipping forward and backward in synchronization as a group. We skipped to the beat of Miss Williams's piano music; our skipping ropes had ball bearings in the polished oak handles.

Later in the program, all the girls and officers took their places on the crowded gym floor while the head officer called out orders: "Right turn, left turn, about turn, forward march, mark time!" Whoever made a mistake went to the sidelines. I was probably eight years old and stayed completely focused on the officer's orders. I found myself the only one left on the floor. I had won the medal. Mother was proud that I was the winner of this feat.

One Sunday afternoon, all of the Boys' Brigade groups, Girls' Brigade groups, Boy Scouts, Girl Guides, Cub Scouts, and Brownies met for a sacred service at Christ Church Cathedral. Each group marched in with special ones bearing the representative flags. The cathedral was packed. Each of the groups walked from the fellowship hall to the cathedral over a covered stone bridge; we could see the street below.

One day at noon, Daddy carried in some large, heavy cartons and placed them on the dining room table. Without taking off his wool overcoat, he opened the cartons and started unpacking a brand new set of Britannica Encyclopedias. I can see him yet, smiling to himself as he took them out one by one, examined them carefully, and respectfully set them down on the table; each volume was individually wrapped in brown paper. He bought some lumber and sheets of plate glass and made a bookcase for the new books in the niche between the dining room fireplace and the outside wall. The wood was quite white where he split it, and he didn't plane or sand it. The completed job looked quite rough. Before long, they called in Mr. Sheeran, our charlady's husband from Killester, who built very attractive lower cabinets with doors and upper cabinets with glass insets on both sides of the fireplace that housed the encyclopedias handsomely. Next, he made built-in wardrobes in the large back bedroom above the dining room. They were built in to the niches on either side of the fireplace upstairs.

Auntie Rene

Grandmother Jennie was forty-seven when Lily came up to her bedroom to ask her what she wanted for breakfast. Granddad Speidel had already gone to work. When Lily came up with breakfast, Grandma Jenny had passed away. Granddad spent a lot of time at her grave and met Mrs. Maud Pennyfeather grieving at her husband's grave. In two years, they married. We called her "Auntie Maud." Daddy and Mother liked her, and she treated us as if we were her own grandchildren.

Auntie Maud was pouring tea. When we were offered a second cup, she poured what was left from our first cup into a small china bowl that matched the tea set. She put a sugar lump in our teacup with a set of small silver tongs; she also poured a little milk or cream into the teacup first before she poured the tea.

Afterward, the meal was cleared away, and Auntie Rene, who was visiting, was sitting in a low easy chair. As we gathered snugly around her, she told us the story of The Little Engine That Could. She had such a musical voice. She and Uncle Willie had no children of their own, and she loved us children and enriched our lives so much with the interest she took in us. Later, she held us spellbound with her story of the little girl who wouldn't get her hair washed. Each time this little girl stamped her foot in rebellion, her nose would grow an inch. The exploits of that growing nose were so funny to us. By the time it grew out across the sidewalk in front of her house and a nanny wheeled a baby in a pram over her nose, the little girl gave in and let her mother wash her hair. Oh, how we loved that story, and oh, how we loved Auntie Rene. What a great mother she would have made.

Mother had some interesting expressions. When she was frustrated about a situation, she would say, "Well, I'm just up a gum tree." When she dropped something while she was busy, she would say, "Crumbs!" If she tripped and fell, she would say, "I came a cropper." She wouldn't talk baby talk to her babies; she talked to them in plain English. Her love names for her babies were "Lovey" and "Chickywicks." When we misbehaved, Mother would say that we were bold instead of saying we were naughty or bad. When we disappointed her in regard to our manners, she would comment, "That is so uncouth."

Daddy had some interesting expressions also. When he was starting to blow his nose, he said, "I need to blow my proboscis." If anything were out of place, he would say, "Let's put all this paraphernalia away." If we were building castles in the air, he would say, "Beggars can't be choosers." If he said something unclearly, he would say, "Well, sounds as if I'm muxed ip." Also, Daddy would say, "If you can't say something good about a person who is absent, don't say anything at all." He also would say, "There are tricks in every trade but ours." Daddy had an interesting way of emphasizing something. If we asked, "Daddy, do you mean that?"

he would answer, "I jolly well do mean that." If Daddy agreed with something he was told, he would answer, "Right you are." If either Mother or Daddy approved of something that happened, they would respond with, "Brilliant!"

One of the aunts gave Audrey Bobby Bear's Annual for Christmas. How we enjoyed reading about Bobby Bear, Porky Pig, Ruby Rabbit, Maisie Mouse, and others. I lost myself in the Just William books and read several of William's escapades.

Mother was reading a lovely book, Little Bruey, to us children. I understandably upset Mother by getting the book and finishing the story. Mother wisely continued to read Little Bruey to all of us anyway. On summer afternoons, Mother gathered us into the dining room and read the account of the building of Solomon's temple. She also taught us about the Ark of the Covenant. Another time, she read to us the book of Leviticus. One of the short songs she taught us went like this:

> Absolutely tender, absolutely true,
> Understanding all things,
> understanding you.
> Infinitely lovely, exquisitely near.
> This is God our Father,
> what have we to fear?

Another verse she taught us was:

> Jesus is the Shepherd
> Guess who I am.
> Such a lovely secret:
> I'm his little lamb.

CLONTARF METHODIST CHURCH

Mr. Brien was the superintendent of the Sunday school. Dorothy Graham, the organist, directed the children's songs for the special children's services. I was still quite young when Mr. Brien told me he wanted me to read a psalm in one of those services. I wore my blue-check, tailor-made coat and matching tam trimmed with blue grosgrain ribbon. I calmly walked up the steps of the walnut pulpit and read the psalm. Mr. Brien thought I did a good job. Audrey, Jean, and I wore matching coats. I can still see the brown oxford shoes that I had received as a Christmas gift.

On Thursday evenings, we children walked to the Clontarf Methodist Church for Junior Christian Endeavor. The church was an artistic grey stone building which was situated on the corner of St. Lawrence Road and Clontarf Road. We sat around the fire in the vestry in a semicircle. Mr. Brien had us take turns reading the verses of a hymn. In "Tell Me the Stories of Jesus," my verse was next. Deliberately, I started, "Skenns by the Wayside." Mr. Brien threw back his head and roared in laughter at my rendition of "Scenes by the Wayside." After scripture and prayer, we played some games in the gymnasium.

One evening after Christmas, I confided to Mr. Brien that I had seen the red sleeve of Santa Claus's coat when he came to our house in the night. When Mr. Brien threw back his head again and roared with laughter, I started wondering if he believed what I had just said.

One spring, Mr. Brien had me take a written Bible examination. I was the only student there. I sat for the Methodist Sunday school Connexional exam. Mr. Brien had me take the test in the vestry. When I handed him my finished exam, he asked me to recite the Lord's Prayer, which I did promptly. I learned later that I was awarded the gold medal, which was first place in all of Ireland.

Mrs. Alfred Collins was the pastor's wife at Abbey Street Methodist Church in downtown Dublin. She started to have me come to her house once each week and trained me for the Sunday school temperance exam. It was very special to sit by her dining room fire as she taught me. I sat for the exam in her living room and was later told I earned the silver medal.

Later, I was chatting away to Daddy while he shaved in the bathroom. "By the way," he began as he looked sidelong at me, "You have been awarded the gold medal for your Bible examination and also the silver medal for your temperance examination. They hope you won't mind if they give you cash instead of the medals." I just loved the burgundy leather purse I purchased. It had two handles and a nice gold clasp that snapped shut. The leather was attractively gathered like a pouch into burgundy-covered clasps at the top. I bought my first pair of fully-fashioned nylons, a soft taupe.

Around this time, Jean and I were having some kind of squabble in the backyard. Mother came out to break up the fight and spanked me. Because I was feeling sorry for myself, I did not know that Jean had been spanked that day too. When Audrey and I had a disagreement, we always resolved this by saying, "We'll settle this at The Judgment."

On Sunday afternoons, we children walked a half-mile to Clontarf Methodist Church because the church hosted Sunday school on Sunday afternoons.

Daddy bought us Arthur Mee's Children's Encyclopedia. Such exciting reading for rainy days: science, history, literature, and art. I loved curling up in one of the easy chairs by the dining room fireplace to read one of those books. I enjoyed the stories, the poems, and the Greek mythology.

One picture that intrigued me was "The Walk to the Sea," which showed the Armenians slowly walking around a mountain after being forced out of their country. Mother said I wore the covers off the Children's Encyclopaedia; she also said when I was reading them, I would not know what else was going on in the room.

Mrs. Sheeran came two mornings each week to help with the washing and scrubbing. Mother washed clothes on Monday, and if they weren't dry at the end of the day, she had a pulley in the kitchen on which she could finish drying the clothes. She loosened a white cord, which let this arrangement of four long, thin, squared poles that were screwed together down low enough to place the still-damp clothes. Then she pulled it up close to the ceiling, where the clothes finished drying out of everybody's way.

Mother had the house cleaned thoroughly every week. I remember the maid down on her hands and knees polishing the dining room floor with paste wax and buffing it to a shine with another clean cloth. The maid scrubbed the pretty green inlaid linoleum in the kitchen after lunch each day on her hands and knees.

Every Monday, Mother pulled the sturdy green Thor electric wringer washing machine out from the corner of the scullery. It was early afternoon before everything was finished, and the washing machine was pushed back to its place near the door that opened into the garage.

Mother baked on Saturday for Sunday dinner. Sometimes she made a two-layer sponge cake with strawberry jam filling. There was no icing on this cake. Other Saturdays, she made "Queen of Hearts," which were a circle of pastry placed in a muffin pan with a spoonful of strawberry jam placed at the bottom of the pastry. She filled each one with a little cake batter and baked them all at once. Other times, she made English trifle. Since I have gotten older and wiser, I think Mother's diet for us was very balanced.

Charlie McMullen, a freckled, red-haired gentleman, stopped his horse and cart at our curb each weekday morning and left six bottles of milk on our front doorstep. His family owned a first-class dairy at the top of Vernon Avenue. A bread deliveryman with an enclosed van stopped by each day to deliver fresh-baked turnovers of white bread. On Fridays, a fisherman with a horse and cart walked down Kincora Road, calling, "Howth Whiting, Howth Whiting." I can still taste that delicious fresh-fried fish.

Mother served us meat for every dinnertime: beef one day, chicken the next, pork occasionally, and fish on Fridays. She bought fresh vegetables from Monelly's grocery and served the vegetables without a cream sauce. She didn't make gravy. She mashed the potatoes in a little of the water in which they had cooked. Sometimes she made parsley sauce to serve over the potatoes; other times, she made creamed onions for the same purpose. These were delicious. Mother served all kinds of vegetables for dinner each day: cabbage, cauliflower, Brussels sprouts, carrots, beets, turnips, parsnips, and peas. She mashed the carrots when they were cooked in a little of the water in which they had simmered. She served a different vegetable each day, and the maid put a generous helping on each of our plates. I love vegetables to this day. Mother didn't serve second helpings.

Breakfast during the weekdays was a dinner plate each of nicely-cooked porridge over which we sprinkled a teaspoon of sugar and poured a little whole milk. I enjoyed the artistic change in the appearance of the sugar when it touched the hot porridge. I thought it was interesting the manner in which the milk encircled the porridge with an even white margin around the edge of the plate.

Some Sunday evenings, Mother served pork and beans on toast. Other Sunday evenings, she served us Welsh rarebit on toast. Sometimes she kept a large wooden crate of South African, light-green, crisp eating apples in her room. She gave us one each day. They were singly wrapped in crisp tissue paper. We enjoyed them so much.

Wednesday-afternoon picnics were egg sandwiches or tomato sandwiches neatly cut in triangles and packed in Mother's square biscuit tins. On Wednesdays, Daddy bought a bar of Cleeve's toffee and had us children share it. One exciting afternoon when I came out of Greenlanes School, Daddy was parked across the road in the green Ford with Mother, the baby, and the picnic supper all ready to leave right then for an afternoon of fun.

The stained-glass windows in our front door prevented Mother from knowing who had used the brass doorknocker to summon her to the door. A gypsy woman was standing there with a place setting of cheap dishes in her hand. The gypsy put her foot in the door immediately so Mother would listen. Later, when Daddy came home from work, I saw Mother cry for the first time in my life as she told Daddy how the gypsy woman forced her upstairs to see if there was anything to trade in Mother's wardrobe. Mother, some way, was able to get her to leave without trading anything, but she was badly shaken by the experience.

Daddy and Mother's bedroom suite had an intriguing dresser. A plate-glass, removable shelf sat low in the center between two sets of deep drawers. Mother's vanity set was a pearled-pink hand mirror and hairbrush. The large dresser mirror was flanked by two hinged side mirrors. I was entranced by adjusting these mirrors gently to figure how many reflections were in the mirror; it was my first encounter with infinity.

Another spellbinder was the water in the bathroom sink. When I put the stopper in, I wondered about the physical makeup of water—when I put my right index finger into the water, my finger completely displaced the amount of water the identical size of my finger. When I lifted my finger back out, the water completely and silently displaced my finger. I hadn't heard yet about molecules, but I wondered why there was no space between my finger and the immediately surrounding water.

One day, I was standing alone, gazing out the large back bedroom window. A tall, deciduous tree stood in the Oulton Road neighbour's yard at the left end of our property. A bright ball of fire whizzed horizontally through the air from the right and flew behind that tree and did not come past on the left side. It did not appear to fly into the tree. What it was or who sent it there remains a mystery in my mind.

We liked all of our neighbours. The Wicklows lived on our side of the road at the corner of Kincora Road and Oulton Road. They were older, quiet, and very refined. One time, they invited David into their back garden. David told us they had a small pond and waterfall surrounded by gardens and brick footpaths. Their back garden was completely hidden from Oulton Road by a tall stucco wall.

The Boyles were a Catholic family who lived next door to our right. The McNultys lived to our left. Next to the McNultys were the Fitzgeralds, who were older, quiet, and very refined. Next to the Fitzgeralds were the Shroedeners, a retired German couple. I was impressed how Mrs. Schroedener placed her sheets and blankets to air out the back bedroom window on rainless days. Years later, we heard that The Prime Minister of the Republic of Ireland, Eamonn DeValera, invited Mr. Shroedener to come from Germany to teach physics in the University of Dublin.

Audrey and I enjoyed visiting with Breege and Sheila, the two older Boyle girls next door. A break in the hedge was made by someone from our family or the Boyle family coming to either house to borrow a cup of sugar or an egg. Breege was taking tap dance lessons, and we liked the patent leather black shoes with the silver buckles she wore when she danced.

Coming through life, I concluded if all the Protestant people in Ireland had treated the Catholic people with the same loving, respectful attitude Daddy and Mother had, there would be no troubles in Ireland.

There would have been no violence or killings such as there were in the North after 1969.

———————————————

Mrs. McNulty had some gooseberry bushes near the cement path by our fence. We children would lie down and reach under the fence and steal her delicious gooseberries. Mother had to put a stop to this. Mrs. McNulty also had chickens at the end of her yard that she fed faithfully each day. Her sister, Miss French, lived with the McNultys. Sometimes I kneeled down by the scullery sink to listen to them say their prayers. I learned the "Hail Mary" this way.

Across from us in a handsome bungalow lived Mr. and Mrs. Ryan. They had a manicured lawn bordered by colorful flower beds all the way around. Mr. Ryan drove Audrey to Wesley College each morning on his way to work.

Beside the Ryans was a two-story white, flat-roofed, stucco house. The entrance to their front garden was in the corner of a healthy hedge. A young man who was still a student lived there quietly with his parents. His name was Oliver; we called him Oliver Twist, of course.

When David was seven, the atmosphere in our house was thick with excitement. After living these years with three older sisters and two younger sisters, David watched Mother bring home a brand-new baby boy from the hospital, Stephen Eric. David finally had a real brother to call his own.

Daddy's three butcher shops were meticulously clean, neat, and orderly. The counter where the meat was sold was made of marble, edged with deeply grained, lightly varnished wood. A tall mirror lined the wall behind the salesladies. The cash register sat in the dead centre. A neat, white, enamel weighing scale sat on either end of the counter. Daddy kept the red needle pointing exactly on zero. He cared deeply about treating his customers honestly. A handsome meat slicer sat on the right end of the counter.

Daddy's butcher block sat against the wall which faced the front door and display window. Daddy wore a suit to work and put on a white butcher's coat and white apron while he worked. On market day, he would carry a whole pig on his back after he had placed a hook in each hind foot to hang it from a steel rail overhead. The first job was to chop it slowly in half from tail end to snout. It swung gently as soon as it was cleft asunder.

One of the clerks scrubbed the butcher block each day with a wire brush and wood shavings to clean it. The terra cotta, red tiled floor was mopped at the end of each day, and fresh sawdust was scattered all across it to keep the tile clean.

The display window in Daddy's shop was attractively dressed each morning. The wide shelf was covered with white ceramic tile. White wrought-iron stands held small glass shelves on which were artistic arrangements of sausages, smoked ham slices, cold, cooked stuffed pork slices, rashers of bacon, and other varieties of pork. The prices were marked with black marker on little white squares of bone that had a pin attached which was stuck into each kind of meat. One of the ladies made delicious pork pies and sausage rolls that were also placed in the display window. An awning was pulled down in the front when shade was needed. A red neon sign hung in the window, advertising "Speidels' Sausages."

A marble countertop was staffed by Phil Grimes, the head clerk, and two efficient helpers. A walk-in refrigerator held all the meats in a room just off the shop. A small cloakroom hid the safe that stood against the locked door, leading up to our family's two-story flat.

Out behind the building was a small courtyard with the break room to the left. The smokehouse for the bacon and hams stood between the break room and the large room where the sausages, brawn, white-and-black puddings were made. Kevin, a hard-working young man, worked out here and also made deliveries to the branch shop that Mary Grimes managed in the Strand. I don't remember if I ever knew Kevin's surname. Kevin also made deliveries to the Clontarf branch shop that Uncle Barton managed, with the help of efficient Miss Fields.

We enjoyed the joke that Daddy brought home one day. Effie Brophy, one of the younger clerks, took an order at the counter and went out to the back shop, calling, "Kevin, have you any brains?" Effie was an attractive, efficient, honest girl whose family were members at Clontarf Methodist Church. We enjoyed having a staff member from our church. I admired the way she dressed when I saw her at the Clontarf Methodist functions.

The accountant, Mr. Reilly, complete with his briefcase, came every week to balance the books. When we children passed him, he would smile at us over the top of his glasses.

One busy Saturday, Mother asked me to take some loaves of bread to the shop to be sliced in the meat slicer. I don't believe she specifically told me to go to the Clontarf shop on Vernon Avenue. I pulled those loaves in a wagon the entire English mile to the store at Marino Mart. Aunt Emily was furious to be interrupted when the customers were packing the store clear to the entrance in their usual Saturday morning fashion. I pulled the wagon under the railroad bridge and passed the attractive residences on my left on Clontarf Road. I hauled the sliced bread all the way home, walking north on Clontarf Road with Fairview Park on the right, passing Malahide Road on the left, then Howth Road, then St. Lawrence Road, also on the left. The inlet from the Irish Sea was on my right, separated from Clontarf Road with grass enclosed by two stout retaining walls. I passed the shops in Clontarf, which included a fine drapery store that was owned by two sisters from Clontarf Methodist Church. Among other stores in Clontarf was a chemist and a bakery that sold the most delicious doughnuts made, without holes in the centre.

Olive Speidel Hall

Clontarf Methodist Church, surrounded by grass and an attractive low, thick stone wall, was on the corner of St. Lawrence Road. I passed Haddon Road and turned left on Castle Avenue and walked up to the hidden castle entrance and turned right. Kincora Road started at the main castle entrance. Two majestic chestnut trees enhanced the entrance; a chain looping evenly between small stone posts was an attractive border around each magnificent tree. Mother was so vexed that I had disturbed the Saturday morning business. She had meant for me to have the bread sliced at the Clontarf shop.

Mary Grimes was Phil Grimes's older sister. Mary was manager of the spiffy shop at the Strand. The Strand shop was fitted exactly like the Marino Mart and Clontarf shops. Everything was clean, shiny, and organized. Mary was an able saleslady. The lunch room at the Strand was always tidy and clean, and Mary was a great manager. Mutual respect reigned between Daddy and all his employees. It was good for us children to know these fine people.

To the right of the Marino Mart shop, a confectioner sold delightful pastries. In the rear left-hand corner of the shop, the post office was housed with a small bank-like opening where the clerk served the customers. Each workday, one of Daddy's salesladies went to the counter at the confectioners and bought two tiny cakes for Daddy's five o'clock tea. When I visited, she bought two extra for me. We must not have stopped in there too much, because I always felt welcome and Daddy never made me feel that I was in his way. We could ride the Malahide bus from Wesley College clear through town over to Marino Mart, stop in and see Daddy, and ride the 44A from Marino Mart to Clontarf Castle.

Sometimes we walked down Oulton Road and rode the number 30, which was a double-decker coming into downtown Dublin from Dollymount. A second entrance to the alley separated the confectioner's shop from the technical school. A third entrance came between the technical school and the chicken and fish shop. Next was McDowell's, a fine drapery shop where Mother bought linens, towels, and dresses from cheery Mrs. McDowell. Beside her shop was the chemist. We pronounced the society these professionals belonged to the "Pharmakyutecal Society," even though it is spelled the same as it is in the United States.

To the left of Monelly's was a fourth alley entrance, and to the left of that was the busy beef butcher. Nothing was ever said about this at home, and we bought all our beef there, but I had a snobby little attitude in my mind that our pork shop was classier. "Costello" was the name placed in wooden letters above the beef butcher shop. Around the curving corner to the left was the bakery. Here they sold the lightest, crustiest rolls shaped like a horseshoe. I loved them.

Abbey Street Methodist Sunday school was putting on a program in conjunction with the Girls' Brigade.

We were dressing up in costumes and acting out some songs. I had to dress up as a gollywog policeman. Mother took me with her to the police station to borrow a police helmet that was identical to those worn by the London police.

In the program, Audrey was a jack-in-the-box. She hid in an attractive box and popped up right on cue. Also, Audrey and I sang a song that went like this:

> I don't want to play in your yard.
> I don't love you anymore.
> You'll be sorry when you see me
> Swinging on my garden door.

Whichever one was singing, she would stamp her right foot on the words want and love.

Audrey, Olive and Jean, 1940

Daddy, Mother and Audrey, 1937

Auntie Rene and Uncle Willie, 1960

Olive walking down a street in Dublin

Speidel family picture taken at home two weeks before we left Ireland

MERRY CHRISTMAS

Christmas was magical for us children. We gathered around the kitchen table and watched while Mother baked the Christmas fruitcake early in December, placing a marzipan layer under the upper white royal icing. She steamed the plum pudding, the top of which was covered with a snow-white square of cloth tied on with a piece of twine. A Christmas Day tradition when friends or family visited was to offer a slice of plum pudding. Nobody's offering tasted quite like Mother's, which had a cake-like texture; she served hers with a hot, sweet cream sauce. We children started the season by writing short letters to Santa Claus. All of us gathered around Daddy's chair in the dining room by the fire. As each one wrote their letter to Santa, telling him what we hoped for at Christmas, Daddy would guide us as we tossed it up the chimney. A few days later, our annual trip to visit Santa in the big stores downtown was a major undertaking.

Mother enlisted Lily's help. Lily had been hired by my grandparents to be nursemaid to Daddy when he was a baby and subsequently stayed on to care for each of the five other children who came later. When they were grown, Lily was asked to stay on as a permanent housekeeper, which she did.

Having Lily along to dote on us was exciting. We first visited Pim's big department store and stood in line with the other children, stretching our necks to catch a glimpse of the wonderful Santa Claus. We were given bangers to play with as we waited. A banger was a triangular piece of shiny cardboard painted in lavender-and-white stripes and folded down the middle, with softer paper attached inside. When we shook it downward, the softer paper would shake out with a bang. When we finally got to see Santa Claus, he reached down by his chair and chose a wrapped gift for us.

Following Pim's, Mother and Lily took us to Brown Thomas's to repeat the same fun, then over to Switzer's to experience the same excitement all over again. Last but not least, we went to Bewley's. Ah, Bewley's! A nice, tall chef was busy in the front display window grinding coffee beans. His tall chef's hat and uniform were of the purest white. We found our way to some adjacent bistro tables inside the restaurant. We each got to choose a favorite sweet cake from the array at the front of the café. I was so intrigued with my cream puff that I didn't notice what the other children had chosen. And then there was a cup of the most delicious, hot, steaming Bewley's coffee, replete with cream and sugar. After all of us had Mother and Lily help us visit the bathroom, we made our way to the green double-decker bus. We climbed the stairs to the top deck so that we could look down on the city while we rode to the stop outside Abbey Street Methodist. We boarded either the double-decker headed for Dollymount or the single-decker, which stopped outside Clontarf

　　　　　Olive Speidel Hall

Castle. On one of these trips, I was so absorbed in the activity on the sidewalk below that I didn't notice that the family had already gotten off the bus until I saw Audrey beckoning frantically from the sidewalk below. I jumped up and ran to the winding stairway and fairly galloped down those stairs before the bus might have started off with one dreamy Speidel girl still on board.

We children woke up on Christmas morning to find filled stockings lying on the bedclothes near the footboard. Santa Clause had come; we had not seen him—such a mystery! We dashed into Daddy and Mother's room to show them what we had found.

"What did Father Christmas bring you?" Daddy would ask, raising himself on one elbow while rubbing his sleepy eyes. After quickly dressing and combing our hair, all of us ate breakfast as fast as we could.

We lined up by ages, youngest to eldest, and went into the magical dining room, which Daddy and Mother had decorated the previous evening with red and green paper chains looping from the corners of the room to the chandelier over the dining room table. Red and green accordion-pleated paper bells hung from the edges of the ceiling. Excitement was running high as we looked for our special group of presents. "I've got a fountain pen," cried Audrey excitedly, picking it out of a lovely new pair of dressy shoes. I leaned in to admire it with her.

"Look over there," Daddy advised. I found I had one too, perched in an equally charming new pair of dressy brown shoes. Fairness always reigned in our household. No hint of favoritism ever raised its head.

One delightful Christmas brought a little drama to our celebration. Daddy opened the pocket doors that separated the drawing room and the dining room. He taped a white sheet to this open space. We placed the dining room and kitchen chairs in rows and sat quietly in the darkened dining room; the lights were turned on in the drawing room. After the dining room table was placed behind the sheet, Auntie Rene walked into the drawing room, groaning with pretended pain. Daddy helped her on to the dining room table while she continued to grown with pain. Daddy lifted his butcher knife and brought it down on the table to the right of Auntie Rene. We thought Daddy was cutting Auntie Rene open. Auntie Rene groaned louder with her lovely, musical voice. Daddy proceeded to pull out lengths of Speidels' Sausages which were obviously the cause of her anguish. We children loved the family joke and the family performance.

One Christmas we four older children each received a nearly new bicycle, complete with a brown wicker basket on each girl's bike. Daddy had polished the wheel rims with steel wool until they were gleaming like new. The two younger girls were given charming new red scooters. When the excitement subsided, Mother came walking into the dining room, pushing a handsome, hunter-green, three-speed, brand-new bicycle for Daddy. Mother's eyes were twinkling with

Olive Speidel Hall

joy; Daddy couldn't speak for a while. She had hidden it next door at the McNultys.

Christmas dinner was unique with a Christmas cracker lying on the table at each place setting and a bottle of fizzy amber lemonade beside each plate. "Pop!" Each child's bottle added to the occasion as Daddy opened each one's lemonade, in turn, around the table. After Daddy returned thanks, we raised our glasses and clinked each other's glasses with our own, which was our way of wishing each other good will.

At Christmas and Easter, Mother had us go to the hairdresser downtown to have our hair set in waves. Each Christmas, she had Audrey and me take a small Christmas cake and plum pudding to one of the tenement houses in the inner city of Dublin. One of Grandmother Price's friends had fallen into poverty and lived with her loyal maid in a basement flat in one of those squalid residences. We held our noses when we entered the tenement house and were always amazed at the cleanliness and neatness of this basement home. The maid was a sweet, kind woman. Her mistress had a peculiar pride that turned me off. One Christmas when we were returning to the bus stop, some boys from another tenement house gave the wolf whistle when we passed.

Another Christmas, Daddy rented a radio and placed it on top of the piano in the dining room. When King George VI gave his Christmas speech, Daddy had all of us stand to listen respectfully.

During the war, families could not find dolls to buy. For Christmas after the war, Mother and Daddy bought each of us girls a new baby doll. On Boxing Day, or St. Stephen's Day, which is the day after Christmas, we girls went crying to Mother, "David has broken our dolls' heads to see how the eyes open and shut."

"Oh!" she responded. "That's just his inventive mind."

Mother's girlhood friend also married a pork butcher. She and her husband lived on Haddon Road, just up the street from Miss Daly's house. Mrs. Stein had two girls our age. We went to church, Sunday school, school, and piano lessons together. The Steins' Christmas party was very special to us. Each year, they had a Christmas tree that stood in the front bay window, decorated with shiny ornaments and twinkling lights. After we had sat down to delightful goodies in the dining room, we sat in the living room in the dark while Mr. Stein showed us a Charlie Chaplin movie. Oh, how we laughed at Charlie Chaplin. Mr. Stein sometimes showed us home movies of their family. Vincent was the youngest child, and I respected him very deeply for his dignity. Mrs. Stein's sister-in-law, Peggy, was a favorite with Ann and Joan. We were invited to her house in Mt. Prospect one day; she had a red tricycle sitting on the patio. For some reason, I chose to ride that tricycle 'round and 'round the patio instead of playing with the rest of the children.

Another Christmas, Mrs. Stein gave me a pink silk lingerie set trimmed with narrow white lace and pink embroidery. At the Abbey Street Sunday school party,

I was sitting in the large windowsill in the small gym, watching the program. I arranged the hem of my dress so that the edge of this pretty pink slip peeked out a tiny bit. I thought it was one of the most beautiful gifts I had ever received.

Mother taught Audrey and me a Christmas piano duet. Audrey played primo; I played secondo. We enjoyed playing "Sleigh Bells" very much. One of mother's cousins was a concert pianist and an adjudicator with the Royal Academy of Music. Mother invited her over to hear us play "Sleigh Bells." Afterward, Cousin May Johnson asked, "Do you try to listen and feel how each other plays?"

I said, "No."

Cousin May counseled, "You really should."

Later, I realized that I had given her the answer I thought she wanted instead of giving the true fact. This was my first understanding of truth.

Mother put the Christmas decorations away on Little Christmas. This is the sixth of January and, in the Christian calendar, it is the Epiphany, or the coming of the Wise Men to see Jesus.

WEDNESDAY PICNICS

Our family enjoyed Wednesday afternoons. When weather permitted, Mother packed a picnic supper, and Daddy drove us to a favorite spot. Daddy played with us, and then we would have our picnic. On one such outing, we were driving toward Howth. A young boy ran out in front of our car and narrowly missed being hit. Daddy braked quickly and jumped from the car, telling us, "I'll teach that boy a lesson." While small Cadbury chocolate bars flew out of his pockets, Daddy caught the boy, turned him over his right knee, and gave him a good spanking. Needless to say, all of us children watched with wide-eyed amazement.

A favorite place to picnic was Enniskerry. Daddy parked the car by a low wall and helped all of us climb safely onto the grass. After a great climb together up and down the hillside, we sat on the blanket and enjoyed Mother's egg or tomato sandwiches. There was usually a baby sleeping in the Moses basket safely by Mother. We delighted in hiking on the meadow across the road, picking primroses and cowslips as we strolled toward the stream in the valley.

A further Wednesday afternoon, we went to a beach. Audrey and I ventured out by some rocks into the surf. We found a cave where someone had built a fantastic castle out of the partly damp sand. It was complete with tiny turrets, a drawbridge, and windows built by somebody with a true artist's eye. We knew when the tide came in the next time that the castle would be washed away. Sadly, we left it to find our way back to the family. But the tide was already coming in, and Audrey and I had to hold on to the rocks as we encouraged each other to be brave. Fully dressed, we pushed, waist deep, against the current and reached our family safely.

Our family was out for a Sunday afternoon drive; we stopped at Portmarnock. Everyone went for a walk, except me; I wanted to stay in the car to read. Jean came running back to put her Sunday hat in the back seat of the car. When she ran back across the road, a car driven by an elderly gentleman knocked her down. His wife was with him in the car; they stopped to help Jean. Daddy came running back. Jean had to rest quietly for days because she had a concussion. All of us tiptoed around downstairs until she recovered. Dr. May checked on Jean in home visits.

Unforgettable Vacations

Each Saturday, Daddy had us gather around his desk. In the bottom drawer, he kept our savings boxes and banks locked. He gave each of us a small allowance, and we put it in our banks to spend on our summer holidays. One summer, Auntie Maud gave each of us about twelve threepenny bits to spend on our holiday; they were bronze and hexagon shaped, more unique than the dime-sized silver ones.

The best thing about summer holidays was that we got to swim, swim, swim. We would swim in the morning, hang our wet togs on the clothesline, and get back into the cold, wet togs to go swimming in the afternoon. I remember my new swimsuit and how much I liked it. Mother bought it at Elvery's, and it was jade with a logo of a swimmer diving on the left and the word Jantzen on the label. I felt so special owning that suit. I can still recall all of us lying on our tummies on the sand while Daddy taught us the breast stroke.

In Greystones, Daddy took us older children crabbing. We began by breaking barnacles off the rocks behind the harbour to use for bait. We tied a small stone to the end of a string and attached some bait. We sat side by side along the pier and dropped our bait down, down, down till it hit the bottom. I had heard about people eating crabmeat, so one afternoon I put a saucepan full of water on the stove and put my crabs in to cook them. The crabs crawled up the sides of the saucepan, pushed up the lid, and it looked at me. I realized I was really hurting them, so I threw the whole pan of water and crabs out on the grass. I think Daddy killed them for me.

In Greystones, the Children's Special Service Mission was a wonderful attraction for us children. The workers built a platform out of sand on the beach. They used shells to make a sign like "Jesus Loves Me" or "God is Love" along the front. Then they decorated the platform and the sign with fresh flowers each day. One of the workers led us in Gospel choruses while someone played a portable organ. Then someone would give a gospel message to the children. We sat on beach towels laid on the sand. The workers stayed in a lovely home some distance from the beach. Sometimes we were invited there to play on the lawn. All of the workers were loving and kind. When they held a children's meeting at the house, we sat on small chairs. At the time I thought I was a Christian. At the end of the message, the lady who presented the talk gave an invitation to come to Jesus. She did such a fine job, I wished I could ask Jesus to come into my heart all over again.

In Poulshone, County Wexford, Audrey and I would sometimes get a picnic lunch ready, and we would walk on the beach to the rocks between Poulshone Beach and Ardamine. Then after our picnic, we walked all the way home. One day, we were more venturesome and decided we would walk to Gorey Harbour, which was the next inlet beyond Ardamine. We had to climb some high cliffs that separated Ardamine Beach from Gorey Harbour. Up we climbed, pulling at the tufts of grass to help us make progress. We were almost at the top when the tufts Audrey grabbed came loose, and she started sliding quickly toward the steep cliffs, which would have meant a terrible fall into the ocean below. To this day, I do not understand how she stopped sliding. I think an invisible angel put out his hand to stop her from falling.

We children were playing in a sandy cove at Greystones Beach. About twenty cement steps led down to this tiny cove. We built a large sandcastle, lined up on a step, and jumped, in turn, into the sandy castle. We were getting up pretty high on the steps, and it was my turn to jump. It looked scary. I turned to the ones behind me. "Don't push," I begged. Of course, the boy at the back of the line took the challenge and pushed. I fell on to the rocks below, head first. Audrey came screaming to help me up, hugging me to her. Blood was streaming from above my right eye. My sisters and girlfriends formed a sorry band as we started to walk up the hill to our rented beach house. One of the girls' mother came running with a tea towel. Then Daddy followed and picked me up to carry me in his arms. I was terrified of being stitched and loudly lamented this fact. Someone stopped his car and drove us to the doctor's magnificent home. She was in residence and honored my request not to be stitched. She cleansed the wound and taped it. She wrapped a white gauze bandage around my head. After several days of bed rest, I was recovered. I wondered for years why it was that when I touched the scar with a cool finger, it felt as though I were touching the top of my head. It was a misplaced nerve, I'm sure. One of the CSSM workers in Greystones came to visit me; she gave me a new book, Daddy's Sword, which I liked so well that I loaned it to a friend, but it was never returned.

DADDY, LAY MINISTER

As far back as I can remember, Daddy was a lay minister with the Methodist Church. Many Sunday evenings, he preached in one of the beautiful, small Methodist churches on the outskirts of Dublin. One evening, he took Audrey and me with him to Kilmainham to sing a duet before he preached. The people in the churches loved my father, and they embraced Audrey and me in their love as well. Another Sunday evening, Daddy took Mother when he preached at Malahide. We children were sitting around the fire in the drawing room while they were gone. Audrey decided to neaten things up near the time when they were to return. She used the Electrolux vacuum sweeper to clean the tile inside the fender where some ashes had fallen. A live ember went into the sweeper and ignited the cloth dust bag. After Audrey doused it with water, we counted the minutes until Mother and Daddy returned, waiting eagerly to tell them how a worse catastrophe might have occurred while they were absent.

The sun had already set. The burgundy velveteen drapes were drawn across the French doors. The sewing machine was sitting in an unusual place by the closed sliding doors that separated the dining room from the drawing room. Daddy was still wearing his navy, wool, plaid overcoat as he stood and solemnly told us the horrible news he had just heard that day. The British and American soldiers had liberated German prisoners that had been locked up in the most degrading conditions in concentration camps in Germany. On the sewing machine, he had placed a loaf of white bread and a bunch of fine bananas. We had known that our bread during the war had been made from day-old loaves that had been broken into crumbs. Now the bakeries had real flour again. Also, during the war, the country had not been able to import bananas. I could not remember how they had tasted before.

During the war, families were given ration books for some of the groceries. Mother shared the coupons for tea with her friends. She had more tea coupons than our family needed.

During these years, David made a homemade go-cart. As we were not allowed to play in the front yard, David would jump on that go-cart, push with his foot, and glide down a well-worn path in the center of the back lawn into the playhouse, gathering speed as he went down the slight incline. He guided the go-cart into a turn to stop himself just inside the playhouse and then pulled the go-cart back up to repeat the same routine over and over.

Daddy ordered a piece of railroad rail. Dublin was taking out the rails for the city trolley system. One of the officials knew Daddy and teased him that Daddy was planning to lay his own railroad in Clontarf to transport his growing family. But Daddy was building a playhouse for us in the backyard; he used the rail for a joist to hold up the roof. Each summer while we were on vacation, Daddy hired his cousin Harry Reid to catch up on any interior or exterior painting that was needed. Harry was putting the roof on the playhouse where his foot slipped on the corrugated-iron roof and dangled. I made up a song about it:

> Oh, Harry fell through the roof.
> He thought it was waterproof.
> Oh, Harry, oh, Harry,
> Oh, Harry, oh, Harry,
> Oh, Harry fell through the roof.

Daddy enjoyed teaching us interesting things about the world. He told us about the Taj Mahal, the Eiffel Tower, and the pyramids in Egypt. He also taught us about the important people in the world: Sir Winston Churchill in England; Gandhi in India; the Shah of Iran, Madame Curie in France who discovered radium; Marie Antoinette and the French Revolution and the Secretary General of the United Nations, Dag Hammarskjold. Daddy told us about King Arthur and his knights and their search for the Holy Grail. I was already grown up when I realized the Holy Grail was the chalice that Jesus would have used at the Last Supper.

Daddy liked to quote the poem "Abou Ben Adhem"; he liked to tell us the story of Ali Baba and the Forty Thieves. Also, Daddy regaled us with stories of how he and his siblings played Tarzan and Jane when they were children.

Because we were Methodists, Daddy told us the story of John and Charles Wesley starting the Holy Club at Oxford University in England. We heard about George Whitfield and Lady Huntington. We loved the stories about John Wesley, especially the one about his being saved from their burning home when he was just a child. He called himself "A Brand Plucked from the Burning."

WESLEY COLLEGE DAYS

A large group of twelve-year-old applicants was taking a series of proctored examinations in arithmetic, algebra, geometry, English composition, European history, world geography, French, Latin, Gaelic, and Bible. We were sitting at individual desks in the gymnasium in Wesley College. The tests lasted for two days. One of the boys sitting beside me dropped his blotter on the floor near me. He had asked me for a one-word answer that he needed for his exam. I quickly picked up the blotter and wrote the answer for him. I quieted my pricking conscience because I had not asked for an answer.

Next morning when we went to school, news was buzzing about one of the girls in one of our favorite families; she had won the nonresident girl's scholarship, which would pay her tuition at Wesley for four years. I had been watching Audrey practice the pipe organ in the lovely stone chapel and was leaving through the oak door when Miss Daly entered the chapel through this same door. Excitedly, I asked her if she had heard that Barbara Stevenson had won the nonresident girl's scholarship. Miss Daly's eyes twinkled when she told me she had already heard.

When I arrived home from school, Mother showed me a letter that had come in the post that day. Wesley College had awarded me the resident girl's scholarship. I was so happy. My parents would not have to pay tuition for me for four years.

At assembly in school next afternoon, the principal, Rev. Gerald Myles, announced all four winners: a resident boy and girl and a nonresident boy and girl. The resident boy was the one who had dropped his blotter by my desk during the exams. The girls beside me were loving and generous with their praise.

During the first day of examinations, we girls were excused to go up to the teachers' lounge. In a very conceited fashion, I remarked to some of the girls that "Cooky" would expect me to win the scholarship. At that very precise moment, Miss Cooke marched in with the sleeves of her graduate robe flying and very angrily grabbed me by the arm and told me, in no uncertain terms, to go back downstairs. I knew she had heard what I had said.

I left my desk during English class to turn in the homework that was due while I had been out taking the exams. Miss Cooke understandably hurt my feelings pretty badly when I was returning to my desk. "You will probably need a bigger hat size to cover that swelled head," she scolded through her clenched teeth.

Mr. Blackman was young and taught geometry very well. But his teacher's black gown was ripped down the left side. A pupil always stood at the door respectfully while a teacher entered or left a classroom.

I stood at the door and told him sincerely that I would be glad to sew up the tear in his gown. He smiled and declined.

The next year, Mr. Peters taught us arithmetic. I held the door for him one day and handed him a Kit-Kat bar in which I had carefully disguised a piece of wood the exact same size as the bar of chocolate would have been. I was a little ashamed when he seemed so pleased to receive it.

Next day, I raised my hand to answer a question. He responded to me first with a twinkle in his eye. "Chancer," he called me, "I met Mr. Devers just down the hall and wanted to share the Kit-Kat bar with him, but it wouldn't break." I knew he liked what I had done.

We had nicknames for most of the teachers. Indeed, we had picked up some of them from my father, who, with the rest of his siblings, attended Wesley College when he was a boy. Miss Mary M. Smith, the head mistress, was dubbed "Mary M." We really liked her, as my father had; she taught us Latin. She would come huffing and puffing in the door, with her teacher's black robe falling halfway down her left shoulder. "Open the grammars to page eighty," she'd puff in her Irish accent. "Porta, porta, portam…" She wrote the date in Latin on the blackboard as soon as she arrived on the teacher's platform. Her sponge eraser was always dampened a little, and she would only swipe part of her chalkings from the board with tired sweeping movements. I'm sure I was still twelve years old when we were translating Caesar's Helvetian Wars.

When I first started at Wesley College, I was placed in Form IB; Miss Abernethy taught us French. I was very impressed that she was planning to see the Passion Play that summer in Oberammagau. We liked Miss Abernethy and instinctively respected her.

While reading a girl's storybook, I was delighted to find that one of the teachers in the story had the unusual name of our Wesley history teacher, Miss Holt. When she had arrived at her desk next morning, I started out of my desk to show her this exciting discovery. I had taken only a couple of steps toward her when her face and ears turned crimson while she screamed at me in a frightened manner, "Go back to your seat!" This was my first eye-opener that controlling a classroom might be a challenge.

We were having a field day, at the junior boys' boarding school, Burlington House. The men teachers were playing the Wesley boys' football team. All the pupils were invited. As the teams played, there we were, yelling encouragement at the men teachers and calling them by their nicknames, even the principal!

Miss Collier was our art teacher at Wesley College. She was a crabby, older spinster. We worked hard with our protractor and compass to complete the geometric drawings and patterns she was teaching us. One day, I took her a freehand pencil drawing I had sketched at home. I had copied an illustration from a storybook of a little girl looking at a daisy she was holding in her hand. I was not trying to impress Miss Collier, but I liked my picture very much and wanted to show my art teacher. I was surprised by her response; she really liked it, and for the rest of my school days at Wesley, she smiled at me when I unwittingly caught her eye.

Wesley College was a Methodist school that prepared students for college or secretarial college. The younger children went to Prep C, Prep B, and Prep A. Then they were promoted to Form IA, IB, or IC. The C classes were for the slower students. Six forms prepared the A classes for college. Form 2A was the equivalent of eighth grade in American schools. Sixth Form had a Head Boy and a Head Girl. After the war, Wesley College welcomed Jewish students.

Tullamaine was the younger girls' boarding house; we practiced hockey on the playing field there. I started Wesley in January just before my eleventh birthday, and Mother bought me a lovely blond hockey stick at Elvery's for a gift. The hockey stick was wrapped on the gripping area with medium-blue rubber. I liked it so much. I was visiting with Daddy at his shop, showing him my pretty new hockey stick. He asked if the new hockey stick would be sufficient for a birthday gift. Remembering that Audrey had been given a Brownie box camera for her birthday the year before, I told him I would like a birthday gift too. I am still ashamed of my greed in that circumstance.

I started wearing glasses at ten years of age. The eye doctor said my left eye was lazy. For a while, I wore a leather patch on my good eye to try to prod my left eye to work. But I would peek through the side of the patch to read because I could not see using my left eye alone. On the hockey field, I didn't see the white hockey ball coming at me. It broke my glasses, and I gained an enormous black eye. Next day, Miss Abernethy, who was also the sports teacher, was giving a pep talk about attending hockey practice. "We all know Olive went to hockey practice yesterday." She smiled at my black eye.

We played tennis at Epworth House, the lovely boarding house for the senior girls. One spring, Wesley put on a field day, hosted at Epworth House. One of the features of the afternoon was a play put on in the drawing room by the Epworth girls. Miss Busy, one of the characters, was represented by an unforgettable performer.

I was asked to help at the bake sale table. I didn't think too much of my job until Daddy came home the next day and told me that I had really used some heavy sales talk on one of his lady customers who had bought a cake. I began to feel guilty and ashamed, until I realized Daddy and the cake buyer were proud of my skill.

One morning in Form IIA English class period, Miss Cooke took us to hear the Radio Eareann Symphony Orchestra as they practiced. The principle player for each instrument performed a short solo. At the end of the session, the orchestra played Handel's "Water Music." I was deeply impressed and thought at that time that the harp was my favorite instrument.

One of our assignments in English class was to memorize "Love Divine, All Loves Excelling," by Charles Wesley. I am grateful; I can still sing it memorized. I'm also thankful for all the poetry we were assigned to memorize throughout my childhood, besides some of the speeches from Shakepeare's "Julius Caesar."

One book that I treasured was a prize I was awarded in Wesley College for achievement in Bible. The book was the Children's Shakespeare by Charles and Mary Lamb. On Saturday evenings, Wesley College showed movies in the gymnasium for the students. Three that I recall were Great Expectations by Charles Dickens, Three Smart Girls, and a travelogue about Pennsylvania.

On February 6, 1952, while we were in drawing class in the gymnasium, we saw the custodian walk through with the British flag in his hands. We were called to assembly and heard that King George VI had passed away. On the radio, we heard Princess Elizabeth take her oath to be queen. I believe she and Prince Philip were on a trip of goodwill to Australia at that time and they had to come home for the king's funeral.

During these years, once each month, Audrey and I rode the bus east of Wesley College to a lady's home. She held a children's meeting for the China Inland Mission. We heard stories about the children in China and prayed for them while we were there.

Mother had a Christian friend who lived alone; we called her "Auntie Carrie." She painted flowers on china plates in her drawing room. A student from Trinity College had boarded with her and was coming back to graduate. Auntie Carrie asked Mother if I would come stay with her while Mr. Charlie Presho stayed in her home during his graduation. I was delighted to attend the graduation at Trinity College and sat with Auntie Carrie. During the graduation, I was amazed at the cat calls which came from the underclassmen when someone they knew walked up to receive their degree. Mr. Presho was receiving his degree to be a Presbyterian minister. Auntie Carrie and I walked behind him up Grafton Street while he carried his graduation robe under his arm. He had his portrait made in a studio at the top of Grafton Street.

I was quite amused at Auntie Carrie when the first thing she did in the morning when she arose was to go through a series of vigorous calisthenics by her bed.

God's Grace

My father conducted family worship in our home each evening on Monday, Wednesday, Friday, and Saturday evenings. Daddy and Mother attended Christian Endeavor on Tuesday evenings at Abbey Street Methodist. We children attended Junior Christian Endeavor on Thursday evenings at Clontarf Methodist Church.

Early each evening, one of the children would open the French door and call out, "All in for read." This meant we would gather around the dining room fireplace with Daddy sitting in his brown leather chair. He laid the open Bible on his left knee and taught us about the Creation, Adam and Eve, Noah, Abraham, Lot, Isaac, Ishmael, Jacob, Esau; he went on to tell us about Gideon and Samson. We enjoyed hearing about David and his mighty men. I have carried a lifelong impression of Isaiah seeing the holiness of God, which is described in chapter six of his book. Daddy used his hands as he taught us; he was a natural-born storyteller. I think he studied for family worship and didn't need to look at his Bible while he taught us. He held us in rapt attention. He taught us about Jesus' life and death, his Resurrection, the Beatitudes, the Sermon on the Mount, Jesus's miracles, and his parables. I distinctly remember the first time I heard about John the Baptist seeing Jesus and pointing to him, saying, "Behold, the Lamb of God, which taketh away the sins of the world." Daddy also told us how the apostles established the early church. He unfolded the missionary journeys of the Apostle Paul. He taught us the faith chapter in Hebrews 11. I loved to listen to him teach us, because he loved us. When he finished with the Bible lesson, we would kneel to pray. One of the most remembered petitions in Daddy's evening prayer was, "Hasten the day when thou shalt reign." We were convinced that Daddy knew that God was real and that He heard his prayer. We children were quiet while he prayed. At the end, on rare occasions, Mother would lead out in singing "Lead me, Lord." All of us children would fall into singing parts as we sang this benediction. Many years later, at the close of Mother's funeral, all of us children sang this prayer a cappella. I didn't know until that moment that I was the only alto singer in the family; we don't have a bass amongst the children in our family, either. Daddy sang bass and Mother sang alto.

In family worship, Daddy also took time out to tell us the stories of Pilgrim's Progress and The Holy War by John Bunyan. In addition, he told us about the early English martyrs: Bishop Latimer, Bishop Ridley, and Lady Jane Gray.

Mother usually had one girl who lived in and helped with the housekeeping. Sometimes she had two girls hired to live in and work. Also, Mrs. Sheeran walked down from Killester twice each week to help with the scrubbing. She would ask Freda if she would like a cup of tea, then she could enjoy one for herself.

I was thirteen when Mother met a Christian girl who was working for another Christian family. Her name was Susan Moore; Mother asked her employer if she could hire Susan. She came and pleased Mother very much. This was the only time I felt jealous of somebody; I thought Mother loved Susan more than she loved me. I remember one day standing by the kitchen door, with my hands on both doorknobs, cruelly telling Susan how much I hated her. Dear Susan was crying—understandably. She was drying the knives and forks and putting them away. Susan must not have reported me to Mother, because I never heard anything about it.

Susan used to sit in on family worship, and one time when she made a comment, Daddy responded by saying, "Susan, you sound like my grandfather."

Daddy's grandfather was John Townley, who lived in Lancaster, England. Each year when Daddy was a boy, their family would go to Lancaster to visit this beloved man. Daddy said he had a shelf of spiritual books lined up above his bed. We heard that he was out driving one Sunday and came across a man who was trying to repair a flat tire. Because it was Sunday, Daddy's Aunt Emily thought he would drive past, but Great-granddad stopped and helped the gentleman fix his flat tire. Another time, we heard that the minister in church announced a bake sale to be held on the church premises. Great-granddad Townley stood up and said quietly, "There's sin in the church, Lord," and promptly walked out.

When Daddy was a lad, he was visiting Lancaster when Great-granddad Townley put his hand on his head and asked him how old he was. Daddy answered, "Eleven."

Granddad responded by saying, "Eric, that is a perfect age to come to the Lord." Daddy came to faith in his early twenties and credited this exchange with his grandfather as the crowning influence on his faith.

Susan was friends with some folk who had visited a church in Colorado Springs. She introduced them to Mother and Daddy. They had some friends who were evangelists, and these people were scheduled to come to Ireland to hold evangelistic services. Mother took Audrey and me up to Rich Hill Castle, where Mr. Finch, with his wife and daughter, Angeline, were staying. Mr. Finch was preaching each evening in a small church in town. Mother was expecting Joy at the time, but she helped with the cooking and dishes at the castle while we were there.

One day, Mrs. Finch had Audrey and me help her and Angeline roll some skeins of yarn into balls. Mrs. Finch left the room momentarily. Angeline leaned over and whispered in my ear, "I like you because you are nice." This broke my heart because I knew I was not nice inside.

We heard that Mr. Finch's brother-in-law was coming in July to hold a camp meeting with Mr. Finch at the Killadeas Manor House near Enniskillen in County Fermanagh. Daddy made plans to take all of us on the train to attend the camp meeting. Susan, Audrey, and I took our bicycles with us on the train.

We stayed in the gatehouse; Susan was with us, of course. We children helped before the camp meeting started by carrying beds up to the rooms and setting them up. We worked in the barn by filling gunny sacks with straw for mattresses. We spent days doing this. We washed windows and cleaned floors. One of the couples who went early to help was the Hoys. Mrs. Hoy directed the assembly of the mattresses. One day, her scissors turned up missing. We found it in one of the mattresses when the camp meeting was over. We dumped out all the straw into the barn, and out came the scissors.

When the camp meeting started, we had services in a large room that had been used for a chicken house. We cleaned this room thoroughly beforehand and put chairs in rows for the congregation. Mr. Finch and his brother-in-law took turns preaching each evening. We children liked Mr. Finch because he played a saxophone while he led the song service. Mrs. Finch played an accordion while she and her husband sang a special song each evening. They sang beautifully together and were a very attractive, loving couple.

The preaching began to get a hold of me, and I started to become smitten in heart when I recalled some of the places where I had broken some of the Ten Commandments. I was going to the railroad station to meet Daddy coming on the train for the weekend. I started early and pulled into a little break by a creek. I had some stationery with me and wrote a couple of letters to my teacher in school and to the Church of Ireland minister's wife. When I visited her daughter, Judy, while she was laid up for a year, I had stolen some of the pears from their pear trees. I hadn't yet reached the railroad station when I noticed the letters were gone from my bicycle basket. I had to retrace my journey and found that I had dropped them in the place where I had written them.

One evening, I tried to find Susan. She was wheeling her bicycle into the gatehouse; she had been up at the manor house helping with the work. I put my hands on the handlebars of her bicycle and sobbed out how sorry I was that I had treated her so meanly. I told her I had been hateful.

She graciously forgave me; I knew she believed me that I was truly sorry. On Thursday evening, during the preaching, I still felt troubled in my heart. When the preacher had finished preaching, I went to the front of the meeting hall to pray. Mother had followed me to the front and was kneeling beside me. I started to pour out my heart to her regarding the house rules I had broken at home. She said, "Olive, tell God you are a sinner." I did not want to do that. I didn't think I was a sinner. However, I lifted my head to tell God I was a sinner, and something broke in my innermost being, and I started to sob.

Just that quickly, the burden of sin fell off my back; I jumped to my feet and said, "I've got it. I've got it." I meant salvation. Mr. Underwood had preached that evening on "the marks of the new birth." When I jumped up and stated that I had gotten salvation, he got up from his seat and came forward, smiling, and shook my hand. Something had really changed in my spirit that moment. I had a new found joy that flooded my whole self. I had no more guilt of sin. I felt the barrier had broken down between all of God's children and me. I wanted to read my Bible and obey my parents. I found I loved God and knew who He was. I had a newfound love for the Bible. I didn't want to be deceitful ever again.

My life from that day has never been the same. I wanted to live a Christian life. I began to realize later in my teens that I would never marry someone who had not been born again. I didn't want to be married to someone who was like me before I was saved. In the Bible, I found instruction, guidance, correction, comfort, and the promise of God's complete faithfulness during the trials, as well as promises of an eternity in heaven.

Atlantic Journey

There began to be whispers at home that Daddy and Mother were considering moving to America.

Mother thought Daddy needed a vacation; so she sent him to visit his sister Madge, who lived with her husband in the Lake District in northwest England. While he was there, God talked to Daddy about buiding an ark to the saving of his household as Noah had in the Bible. Another Scripture verse which led Daddy is recorded about Abraham in Hebrews 11:8, "he went out not knowing whither he went."

An older couple from America came to visit us. Daddy and Mother made a trip out of town to speak with the pastor of a church in Colorado Springs. Grace Tabernacle was connected with an exclusive Bible college that also had a grade school division and high school division.

The pastor gave Daddy and Mother a school catalog. We studied the classes offered, and the attractive, glossy, black and-white pictures of the faculty, the student body, the band pictures, and the chorus pictures appealed to me greatly.

Daddy went to the Cunard White Star Line and booked a passage for eleven of us to leave in November. Our beloved housekeeper, Susan Moore, had agreed to come with us. The older couple that had visited us were ranchers from Campo, Colorado, and they wanted to be our sponsors, which meant that if we got into financial problems when we arrived, they would be there for us. By the grace of God, we didn't need to use their offer.

All of us visited the United States consul, who approved of us as immigrants to the United States. He issued visas for each one of us. Each of us had to be vaccinated against smallpox and to have passport pictures taken.

One of the most exciting moments was when Uncle Willie and Auntie Rene came to take us four older children for a short tour of Dublin before we left. They took us to St. Michan's Cathedral, where we saw three mummies in a crypt under the church. We went to Trinity College to see the Book of Kells, one of Ireland's National Treasures. This consists of the four Gospels handwritten in Latin by monks in a monastery; each capital letter at the beginning of a chapter is ornamented with flowers in color. We went to Christ Church Cathedral and went below to see the dungeons underneath. The guide turned off the lights for a moment so we would understand what thick darkness was like. We climbed Nelson's Pillar and looked out over Dublin. We went to Wesley College to tell Mr. Myles good-bye. He shook hands with each of us. I was so hungry when we got home that I forgot to wash my hands before dinner and was aghast when I later remembered I had shaken hands with the mummies under St. Michan's.

Daddy bought some brand-new musical instruments to take with us. He wanted us to participate in the school band. He was not allowed to take all of his money out of Ireland at one time, and buying the instruments there resolved that issue in a small way. He bought two French saxophones—one for Audrey and one for me. He bought two trumpets—one for Jean and one for Enid. He bought a trombone for David and an alto horn for Freda. Mother had Mrs. Hoy make tan canvas covers to protect the lovely new instrument cases.

Mother and Daddy scoured Dublin and found thirty-two used trunks. Granddad Speidel built a box for Daddy's books. We could see that Granddad understood Daddy's love for all of his books.

On the day we left 32 Kincora Road, Enid kissed some of the interior walls good-bye. We had had such a happy home there. We gathered at Amiens Street Station to catch the train for Cork. Auntie Lillian was there to tell us good-bye. She gave me a lovely red leather writing case with a shamrock embossed on the front. When the train pulled out of the station, Mother started to cry; she thought she may never see her older sister, Auntie Lillian, again. I had hardly ever seen Mother cry; I started crying too. Jean told me years later that she was crying too. Daddy didn't try to stop us; he was comforting Mother. Soon, I was able to stop myself. Pretty soon, Mother realized, in the excitement of leaving Dublin and her older sister, she had failed to notice that she had left the baby's diaper bag on the railway station platform. She had to wean the baby from her bottles and her diapers while we journeyed across the Atlantic. Mother was one brave lady.

We reached the city of Cork, County Cork, in late afternoon. Daddy found a restaurant for us to eat supper. We waited at the Cobh Harbour for our ship. When we saw the lights come over the horizon, we were tremendously excited. The Georgic looked like a floating city. We boarded a ferry and rode quite far out into the deep to meet the fantastic ship. Some folk were leaning over the rails far above while they observed us boarding; they had probably boarded in France or England. We went in through a door that was opened on the side. We went straight to the dining room for a breakfast of bacon and eggs at one thirty in the morning. Immediately, the faint drone of the engines and the gentle rocking of the ship made me seasick. We had two cabins. Mother, Daddy, Baby Joy, David, and Stephen each had a berth in one cabin. Right next door, we five girls and Susan each had a berth in the next cabin. A nice porthole was on the seaside of each cabin. A sink with running water was in each cabin.

The meals were wonderful. There were two sittings for each meal. We were served at second sitting. All of us could sit at one table. We had two of the nicest waiters who served constantly. Daddy let us choose our own meals. Stephen, who had just turned five, was really struck with the sound of Salisbury steak and princess pudding. He ordered them for breakfast, lunch, and dinner. One evening, my scoop of ice cream tasted so good I asked Daddy if I could order a second helping. He approved. I enjoyed that one so much I asked if I could please have a third helping. I saw the waiter wink at Daddy, and Daddy smiled. The waiter brought three scoops in my next dish, and I ate every spoonful. Oh, it tasted so good, and I was satisfied.

Each morning, the steward came in to make our beds and vacuumed the floor also. Of course, I couldn't resist teasing him and would pull the electric cord out of the wall socket, not once but twice. After two or three spells, I saw I should stop teasing him and let him get on with his work. He was a hard worker, and we respected him.

All of us had a taste of seasickness, except Daddy and Susan. We liked to sit on the deck chairs sometimes. One morning, I saw this beautiful lady far down the deck leaning over the side, throwing up her meal. Her handsome husband was comforting and supporting her. Pretty soon, she recovered, and they started walking down the deck toward us, arm in arm. They were Mother and Daddy! I hadn't recognized them at first; I had forgotten that Mother had a new brown gabardine coat. I was so proud this handsome couple were my very own parents.

One night, we encountered a storm at sea. We could hear the deck furniture crashing around upstairs. We girls doubled up in our bunks so we wouldn't be tossed so much. We heard the baby's only bottle fall on the floor in Mother's cabin and roll against the wall.

The ship turned around and retraced the journey for one whole day, which made us two days late arriving in New York.

Mother had become friendly with a Catholic lady on board. The morning after the storm, she mentioned that she thought Mother and Daddy were probably down on their knees praying during that awful storm. Mother responded, "Indeed, I don't think God told us to take the family to America, only to dump us in the Atlantic Ocean."

The Georgic was a tourist ship with only one tourist class, so we could go anywhere on the ship. It had only two big black smoke funnels instead of three. We could play badminton on the top deck. Sometimes a Scottish bagpiper stood up there and played his pipes. At that time, I didn't like the bagpipe music.

We docked in Halifax, Nova Scotia. Stephen was with me. I thought he would like to see all the goings-on down on the deck, so I lifted him up and set him on the edge of the ship and held him securely while we both watched the people moving about below. Pretty soon, Audrey came up and scolded me severely for putting Stephen at such risk; she told me years later that Daddy gently reached around Stephen and me and took Stephen down from his perch. I still know he was perfectly safe with me.

We sailed on to the New York Harbour. Daddy got all of us up early the day we expected to dock. At 5:30 a.m., we were all standing by the rail as the ship sailed slowly passed the Statue of Liberty. We felt such respect for her and knew it was a special moment for our family.

When the ship docked in New York, Joy was ill with a rash and fever. Our family had to check with a doctor before we were allowed off the boat. Because of Joy's illness, there was the distinct possibility that we might have to go to Ellis Island instead of going on to Colorado Springs. Audrey was beside herself with worry. The doctor approved that we disembark in New York. We were so happy and excited. As we went down the gangplank, I impulsively ran ahead. I raised my right arm and shouted delightedly to the rest of the family, "I am first on American soil!"

EPILOGUE

Daddy contracted multiple melanoma and bone cancer in February 1959. After major surgery that showed that the lymph nodes were clear, Daddy lost his battle to cancer on August 21, 1960. His last day in church was to walk Audrey up the aisle for her wedding.

Mother courageously found work as a bedside caregiver to round out the income. The doctors admired her skill in caring for elderly surgical patients. She lived until a few days after her eighty-seventh birthday. She always kept a thankful spirit. She stayed with one of us girls for three months at a time before moving to another. She was so easy to please. She asked her doctor if she could move to a nursing home when she was almost eighty-two. All of us were with her when she passed away.

Except for Joy, each of us children has made one trip back to Ireland in the years since we left. When Audrey and her husband visited, they knocked on Boyles' door; some of them were home, which led to a lovely reunion. Since then, Breege has visited our family in Colorado Springs, and all of us stay in touch with her at Christmastime. Breege is a successful nun in California.

In the years since Mother's death, when we girls are visiting, someone will invariably say, "We had such a good Mother." That goes for Daddy too.

End Notes

1   http://northstrandbombing.wordpress.
com Dublin City Archives, Eibhlin Byrne,
Mayor of Dublin, Ireland, 2009

2   Ireland, A Terrible Beauty by Jill and Leon
Uris, Bantam, 1975, New York, NY

3   Compton's Enclopedia, 1968
Edition, Ireland, pg. 288